DANIELA ANDONOVSKA TRAJKOVSKA

ELECTRONIC BLOOD

Daniela Andonovska Trajkovska

ELECTRONIC BLOOD

Translated from Macedonian into English language:
Daniela Andonovska Trajkovska

KARAMANOV NATIONAL PRIZE FOR POETRY
2019
Republic of North Macedonia

Premio Mondiale
"Tulliola - Renato Filippelli" in Italy in 2021

**DANIELA
ANDONOVSKA TRAJKOVSKA**

ELECTRONIC BLOOD

2021

ISBN: 978-81-8253-779-8

First Edition:
2021 Rs. 200/-

Cyberwit.net
HIG 45 Kaushambi Kunj, Kalindipuram Allahabad - 211011 (U.P.) India http://www.cyberwit.net
Tel: +(91) 9415091004
E-mail: info@cyberwit.net

Printed at VCORRE PRESS.

heart line

PRESERVED DREAMS

we easily forget what has been written
in the book of life
and we are running and running
around the leaden letters of extrinsic time

and when with a face all in sweat
and with hands in paint
before the alarm in us speaks we will look
in the eyes of that book
the book that we are writing all by ourselves
between the old yellow paper sheets
we will recognize
pressed chamomile meadow

and then we will remember
that we have played Loves Me Loves Me Not many
times before
by pulling the white petals of the day
so we could know whether the chosen ones loved us
although we know now that they have never loved us

and we would fall asleep peacefully

with a winded up time and a pillow stuffed with dried dreams
we will be waiting for the new springs
in the dreams
of our nothingness

DESERT OF THE SOUL

the eagle in flight
cannot see the sand grain,
but the desert sees it
- with all of its salted grains and oasis

TEACHER

the green table hung on the gaze
of the little starry nights
has bloomed the roses
in the yard of my family house, too
it tickled them on their stomach
and stole their thorns

PAIN

Time lives in us in pain
Because of the pain we get up in the morning
to be one step away from death

HEART LINE

with an unexpected glimpse
it peeled me off my palm
that old heart line
on which my body springs
as it is on hot wire
that lives in endless pain

SISYPHUS

I've been hitting the post all my life
and my tendon always comes back to me
all in rapture

The seconds keep rolling me
uphill and downhill of the day

DRESSED UP FACES

when the walls are moving toward each other
to squeeze the air from the room that we live in
I am not mad at them…
they don't know the other way

and when the masks are putting their faces on
themselves
to show that they are always right
I am not mad at them either…
they have no faces

and when they revenge on the bread
even then I am not mad at them…
I know that they see with their eyes only

when I can't get into my room with sticky walls
on which many hung faces look at me
I slam the door and get out of my skin
and then I get mad…
I am mad at myself
I am mad
because I don't know how to be mad

DECISION

The door has closed.
The windows are about to blow.
The air seeks for a hole
to get out,
but the express pot
has already made a decision.

ASH

on the edge of the little coffee table
a mirror was playing
with the reflection of the day,
while with a triple thread
the spider was trying to stitch the word
crumbled the other night
so it wouldn't rest between the seams
of the wooden floor

the fire in the hearth was coughing
in the rhythm of the hand raising

in the room
in the middle of the sleepy fire
in the middle of the torn word
in the seams of the soul
it started to smell like something has been burnt

and while the tongue was tasting the black
the thought was getting into the frame by force
in the frame in which the pain
was dreaming about ashes

HUMAN CIRCLE

the young man
bended and blew in the face
of his newly born son

the maple tree in the yard
leaned on the young man's shoulders
and poured all of his years
in his lap

the old man gathered what was crumbled,
put it in his chest
and immured himself in the little room
under the eyeless house in the yard

arythmics

ARHYTHMICAL SIGH

a female sigh
that was ripped in the middle of the night
stretched on the four sides of the bed
so she could put her displaced upper back
in its place,
washed her face
and continued to live
in the second part of the dream
in the moments of having a hot shower
after which she was combing her hair
in front of the mirror
without any present thoughts
when she was driving on the same road
from home to school
when she was silent in the amphitheatre
where the chairs were solving
the unsolvable riddle
when she was talking endlessly
while she was explaining the theory of creation
although she couldn't know either
whether from the beginning
her story had started

when she was driving from work to home
and when she was having a hot shower again
with arythmical music in her ears
so she could shake
the humped gazes of the day off her body
when after she had had lunch
she was shaking off her thoughts
along with the leftovers
as she was putting the table
in place
when immediately after that she would sit
behind the steering wheel
in order to drive the other people's desires
when she was excercising Tae-Bo
with the women without faces
when she was coming late home
with increased muscle mass,
but with lack of magnesium
when she was going over the walls
with the vacuum cleaner
so she could capture the spiders of the night
when she was hanging the clothes
on the clothesline of the sky
when she was calculating Chi-square result
on the keyboard of her life

before she could get some sleep
for at least three hours
like a normal sigh

a female sigh
that was ripped in the middle of the night
stretched on the four sides of the bed
so she could put her displaced upper back
in its place

REMINDER

there is a rock that I pass by every day
I find it in my bed very often
when I wake up in the middle of the night
and put my leg on the floor
so I could be certain that it is here
and I fall asleep again

sometimes it is standing
in front of the door
and is waiting for me
to come back from work

sometimes I find it in my backpack
with my laptop
and before I start to write
about my sleepless nights
I put it on my desk next to the dried hopes
of my midlife

there are moments when I forget about it
and when I feel its gaze on my body
I got chills instantly

and I my body starts to shake off
the calcificate of my consciousness

there is a rock that I pass by every day
but it keeps coming back in my palm
so I could be awake
when I am about to happen

FUNCTIONS OF LANGUAGE

In the moment when the two ends
of the communication wire were trembling,
although the first one with fast oscillations,
and the latter one with slow oscillations,
the word got stuck in the universe's neurons
to make the connative function of the language happen

the dot that was oscillating slowely
turned off the Wi-Fi of her mobile phone
and then she turned off the phone as well,
just in case,
so she could dream about her previous birth

when she woke up the next morning
the words that were never spoken
hugged each other
and that is how the poetic function happened

referential function[1] was a catalyst

---

[1] There are 6 function of the language according to Roman Jakobson: referential, emotional, connative, matalinguistic, poetic, and phatic function.

for the fire that was burning
in the nucleus of the word
And when she looked at herself
in a mirror one day
the slow oscillating dot saw a dot
that was in extremely high frequency
and then she understood why she had recently had blurry
vision
and why the eye drops were nothing
but a water that cries
and when the media started to sleep
during the night,
and have a nap during the day
and when the idea stayed
in the head of the Sender
and when the presence of the word
was telling a story without a main character
without an action and an opponent
then the eyedrops started to have an effect
and the referential function
was replacing the emotional function unnoticeably

reflexive function
became justifiably proud because
the phatic function died,

although the referential function
has never been more alive

the connative function was capturing
the seconds of nonexisting time with its pupils
from time to time
long enough for the synapses of the nonsleepness to be filled
in the poetic function of the language

DROWNED CHRYSANTHEMUM

in the manhole in which all capital cities
are gathering the telephone calls of the melancholy,
the photoshop of the soul,
the holograms of the lost youth,
the SMS of the short dates
and the cracked valley
of the simultaneous e-messages,
the yellow chrysantemums of the flower girl
sleeping on the square of the looks
drowned

it was surprisingly to see them rising
in the two-dimensionality
of the carcinogenic time
in which we drink virtual coffee each morning
and we eat cake from the folder of emoticons and
stickers

STICKER FOLDER

make the orchid in the living room
bloom
with a glimpse
because it is yours

but you keep breeding chrysantemums
in the folder of stickers

ELECTRONIC LIFE

our days are living
in the electronic messages
that grow on our fingers
like nails with which we scratch the door
that keeps us closed
- each of us in its own autistic room

we depend on the transfer-rate
of the communication link
the most important thing to us is to know
with how many megabits per second
we pass from one part of the story to the other
and how many megabytes we have
to memorize ourselves with high resolution
on the fake image that no one notices
between the shape without a content
before the RAM memory of our sour time
erases us

ELECTRONIC QUADRIPEGICS

I wonder how long could we live
without the electronic lungs
on which we are stuck with a body that it is not ours
– quadriplegics with infrared light in our head
without the vacuum cleaner with which we collect
the spider web in the corners of our consciousness that it is not allowed
to go out without face powder
without the bulb that we bow to
as if it was God of the Sun
without the bread making machine
that feeds us with gluten and additives
with E-215 code
because it can't hit the table with the dough
to soften the stone heart of humanity
so that we could understand that
this is the only way
to capture the air as an additive
of ancient times
without which we are nobody and nothing
without the megapixels with which we see

the world
and without which we are blind
without Wi-Fi that enables us to speak
all the languages at the same time
and with which we are knowledgeable,
but not wise,
famous faces that live in a can
how long could we live without
the flow of electronic blood
in our facial blood vessels
without the chipped democracy
that carries us in its pocket constantly
so that it could call us in necessity
to set itself free

CHIPPED DEMOCRACY

we keep the chipped democracy
in our pockets
so we could imprison the moments
and translate them in megabytes
that we share with the people
who don't know anything about us
and they don't even care if we exist

we are all the same – cloned identities
in the zero-one time

EUTHANASIA

don't listen to the robot in me
that speaks all the program languages
and can do all the mathematical operations
without a mistake
and kill him with euthanasia

sometimes you have to die
if you want to live

LIFE AND DEATH

sometimes it's good enough
to tell someone that he is dead
so he could remember that he has been alive

sometimes even the death of a human
is not enough
for the humanity to know that it is alive

sometimes it's good enough
to look at the clock
that winds up our steps on the back
and to see that we have never lived before

and when all clocks will show the same time
all people will remember that they are one
and then all lives will be born in death
so they could live us

ELECTRIFIED DESIRES

we don't cut the cuticles
that leave their heads in our electrified desires
as ticks do
we don't even trim the nails
to have them under control behind the bars
of the computer keyboard
we don't even file them to protect ourselves from
scratching
while we write down the passwords
with which we enter
the three gates of our single cell
in which we are keeping our freedom so passionately
just for ourselves
we are alone – in between the automatic electronic
messages
whose endings are all the same
and the life that keeps failing to begin

TROPHY HEADS

we are drowning
in the autistic time of trophy heads
that are being willingly beheaded
and posted on Instagram
in order to be part of the mosaic
that falls apart in the moment of creation

dear God, please erase
our two-dimensionality
and put us together on the picture
in which we would live in all of our dimensions

ELECTRONIC COIL

our genes are tedpoles in the endless sea
in which the codes of time sleep

with electronic coil
we are imprisoning life
but life dies once a month anyway
all in blood and in stomach pain
and we put a nameless tombstone
there
because no one wants to know
where hisown life rests
nor that there is no life
because it's easier for us to not know
that our life has died

we are zombies with illusion of God
in the middle of the madness of zeros and ones

wake up the time in us, oh God,
and let us flow in the river
one more time
before we return home

THE COMPUTER UNDER MY SKIN

The computer under my human skin
is never on stand by nor on sleep
and it's never in a mood for conversation or for a play...
but I always forget that
the metal particles are dumb
because they have never been children
and I am angry with myself for talking to them in the first place
as they can understand the child in me

MARGINS

in the margin we live our best lives
because we were born free
and we die free there
in every awakening and every falling asleep

there are no media nor evil eyes
that are magnetically attracted
to the centre of the elite poverty of the soul

there are no masks to parade
in front of the Sun King
so they can be what they will never be

Everyone is afraid of the margin
because the margin speaks aloud
the words that the government will never say

the margin only is sentenced to life in prison
in between the eyes full of letters
and the lead rested in stone

in the margin we live our best times

because we know that we are only time travellers
and we cannot take anything from this world
except for ourselves

LOVE OF THE FLAT EMOTICONS

I can't write a love poem
with the language of the emoticons
(hi babe☺, bye sweet heart☎, tnx, I Luv U)
a poem without cellular love in it
I can't write a poem
about the shadows that jump around
on the techno music of the alienation.

He tells Her He loves Her with a drink
so He could look at Her face
and see His growing Ego
bought in the gym of fake sighs,
and She confirms She loves Him in one gulp
so She could live in the gossips from other people's lives
while Her future is having a ride
in His Bentley.

I am not able to write a love poem,
nevertheless, I wrote a poem
of the flat emoticons' love.

ELECTRONIC LOVE

love is on sale
in the shop windows of desire
in the Book of Faces
where everyone is taking a selfie
with the duck face of despair
as a pop-up of the melancholic everyday
in the society
in which everything can be bought
for only 2.99 euros at a 50-percent discount—
but the soul is what's really reduced.

FACELESS FACES

He and She were sitting on the iron spring
in the two-dimensional reality
with illusion of 4D
and each of them on their-own side
with electronic blood without a security token,
but with a dot at the end of the sentence
was concealing
the Thing that was standing between them
while It with the voice of the margin
was trying to attract attention to Itself
so It could say
that the Thing that is standing
between Him and Her
has its-own profile
in the Book of Life
without any likes
nor sharing
and without any live streaming
and without posting
of the naked conversations
of the depression…

The Thing that was living
between Him and Her
had no name, nevertheless
It was the most common noun of contemporaneity

PERSONS

1. FIRST PERSON PLURAL

First Person Plural lives
only in the ancient stories
without singular forms
without conjugation
without family name and
migration

2. *SECOND PERSON*

Second Person Singular and Second Person Plural
have two faces
The first one lives on the forefinger of fear
and the latter – on the lifted shoulders of
the postponed time
that never knows what it wants

Both of them have no human faces

3. THIRD PERSON

Third Person Singular posts on its timeline:
“Checked in Prague”
“Feeling loved with MN”
“BM is feeling motivated with RGR and 3 others in Ohrid”
selfie#girl#Friday#bali#ocean#water#blue#pool#love#longhair#look#luxury#blackbikini....

Third Person Plural posts on its timeline:
“visit of the homes of the citizens...”
“intensive reconstruction of the ring road...”

Third Person Singular and Third Peson Plural,
it doesn’t mean that they are two persons
- they are both advertizing themselves
on the left click of the sold time

4. FIRST PERSON SINGULAR

only Third Person Singular and Third Person Plural can
be forgiven:
blind interpunction and
“bali” instead of “Bali”
and false check-ins in hotels
and puffed grins with impersonal eyebrows
and bursted emoticons
and flags turned upside down
and transparents all in disguise
and tongue split in half

that is why no one speaks in first person singular
today

(electronic) blood

GENTLE ROUGHNESS

As much as I love my words
I want you to throw me on the bed roughly
and to tear my phonemes and sememes

make love to me only
because my body is not capable of lying

BLOOD SPOTS

drops full od captured breathing
are rolling down my body
after we have created
new blood points
on the coordinating system
of our dreamful time

WHITE WORDS IN A RED SKY

when we join our thoughts
so we could exchange electrons
that willingly tear apart of their skies
so they could love new gravitation of protons and neutrons
our cells start to breathe as one
- with mixed blood of white words and a red sky
they are being born again
on the shore of the new land

CIRCULATING NIGHT

The blood cells of your time
and the blood cells of my time
breathe in the sweaty drops
of our transparent bodies
that exchange anions and organic ions
in the coordinating system of silent words
before they burst loudly in the night
that circulates in us

WE ARE SLEEPING ALL DRESSED UP

our sky only is seeded with stars
that look at the window of our foggy house

we are sleeping all dressed up
me – under your skin, you – under my skin

BIRTH

in the expectancy of the night
we pull out the acute angle of our chests

you are laying down on me
I am being born in the zero

WE BREATHE TOGETHER SO WE COULD BE OURSELVES

on the sky we draw
coordinating system of chromosomes

we breathe together
so we could be ourselves

COSMOPOLITIC LOVE

I'm attending a science conference in Brussels
and on the white screen
behind the European Commission
I read the speech of our interwoven bodies
and then in the watery drops that are being rhythmically
exhaled by the ionisator
I find my home…

You are waiting for me in the office
in which on the same meridians and parallels
The Eiffel Tower and Sahara are hanging,
and the Great Canyon dips in the glass
on which your breathing reflects –
with your little finger you build our cottage
in Arizona forest

Our thoughts living on the skyscraper
of the dreams are kissing passionately
over the seat and the soul of Europe,
over the Equator
and over the greatest hole in the Earth
for which almost no one knows

that it is the womb of the human life itself

In a little cottage in the middle of nowhere
between the European Council,
the desert of the hunger and the world's eyes
on our white bodies
with naked fingers and tongues
we are drawing the new geography map
of the risen world

NAKED

I want you to see me
as I see you
no address
no names or initials
no titles nor attributions
no make-up nor clothes are allowed

I want you to see me naked
because I wear my skin perfectly

WEDDING

I am your wedded wife
united with you in the eternity

on the ring finger
the unwedded rings are getting unwed

the eternity awakens in me
and I wed your soul in me

like every time before
and every time in the future

CONCEIVED SILENCE

when you are losing yourself
in the breathing of my universe
and your words are making me conceive
the silence in my sky
I vanish between the pages of the night as well
bodylessly I rebirth myself in you

NONSLEEPING DREAM

I fall asleep
with a drop of dew on my body

inside the drop
your nonsleeping dream
breathes

DISTANCE

between my fingers and your fingers
the loudest silence lives

between my thoughts and your thoughts
the words are flowing down like electrons

between my lips and your lips,
the space becomes a dot

OVERLAPPING

Overlapping.
The clock hands
are longing for overlapping and
for being close to each other
and for becoming the other

when the clock hands meet
the love is celebrating the overlapping
of the two time travellers
and then -
drinking the glass that is resting on the nightstand
to the bottom
leaving the glass
upside down without a bottom
undressed
speechless
when with one of its hands
the time will go through the skin of the glass
without sobbing
breaking the glass into pieces
on the floor.

And then –
passing by each other
outrunning each other
leaving one after the other
ignoring the night spent together
the day before
overlooking the clock hands
having no memories about the glass.

The night covers itself before it goes to sleep:
an alibi is resting on the surface of what had never
happened before
and will never happen again

THREADS

When I was born by the poem
with crumbled words of silence
and when the threads of death I was tearing and throwing
beside me on the road
and when with my head
I was rupturing the membrane of life
I didn't know that in the womb of the century
my grand grand mother was holding
new threads in her hands for me

with the needle of her breath
she is still sewing them on my feet

INSIDE ME

dedicated to my grandmother

when you came into my dream
with the face of an angel
that is longing to see its reflection
in the mirror
and when your thought
was seeding the words of wisdom
on the red soil of my maturity
and when with the warmth of your breath
you were holding the walls of my house
I have never thought
that I would lose you again
even in my dreams

And then after so many salty rivers
that were flowing from my soul to your soul
I eventually understood
that the more you are not here
the more you are here

Inside me

THE WORLD IN A DOT

dedicated to my grandmother

when with your braids
you were tickling my thought
and when with the river in the look
you were showing to me
where the birth pain flows
and with the cracked palms of the soil
you were teaching me how to be strong
and when with the honey words
you were unlocking my heart,
then my pupils became a homeland
for the whole world
that all of a sudden fell asleep
until the next burst in explosion

SUPERNOVA

dedicated to my son

your smile
under my left heart valve was born
with my thought I kissed your little head
while your tiny leg
was making footprints
in the universe inside me

I was peeling the crust of the oblivion
every day
while I was preparing the cradle of recognition
so you could look at me
with the eyes of my soul
before you cry out loud:
Mama...

A LOOK

dedicated to my daughter

You looked at me
with the salty water of my soul
and you instantly wash out the birth pain

I was tearing apart every piece of the sky
for which I believed that could conceive
and I was breathing inside the word
that had the most significant sematic value
when even unspoken
from the sunflowers' house was wringing
before it ran and tickled the bare feet
of the white pigeon
that keeps our dreams at light

I RECOGNIZED YOU

In the lightnings of the dream
I recognized you
for you naughty words
in the dilated pupils of the ocean
full of salty bubbles

I saw you
after you left me the legacy of your breath
because your own blood couldn't recognize
the genius in the black humour of your life,
nor in the rainbow hidden in the spiderweb

And for the stabbed knee I recognized you
from which the red blood cells of the music flowed in
the picture with scattered brushes
in which the life
our life
has begun

THE GREEN LOVE

the green color of your body
was composing the life out of the cage
and my footprints
were circling on a daily basis
hitting the framed look of the day

a woman opposite the building was observing
the balcony with red pelargoniums
each evening
while the green bird was threading tirelessly a human
hair
into the keyhole that has never been locked
and there inside a yellow domestic canery with a beak
outside the cage
was learning to sing without musical notes
written on the cookbook

SHORT BIOGRAPHY

Daniela Andonovska-Trajkovska (born February 3, 1979, Bitola, North Macedonia) is a poetess, scientist, editor, literary critic, doctor of pedagogy, university professor. She works at the Faculty of Education-Bitola, St. "Kliment Ohridski" University-Bitola, Republic of North Macedonia and teaches the courses: Methodology of Teaching Language Arts, Creative Writing, Critical Literacy, Methodology of Teaching Early Reading and Writing, ect. She is co-founder of the University Literary Club "Denicija PFBT UKLO" and also of the Center for Literature, Art, Culture, Rhetoric and Language at the Faculty of Education-Bitola. She is a member of the Macedonian Writers' Association, Macedonian Science Society – Bitola, Slavic Academy for Literature and Art in Varna – Bulgaria, Bitola Literary Circle, and she was president of the Macedonian Science Society Editorial Council (for two mandates). She is editor in chief of the literary journal "Rast"/ "Growth" issued by the Bitola Literary Circle, and also - editor in chief of the International Journal "Contemporary Dialogues" (Macedonian Science Society), and editor of "Literary Elements" Journal (Perun Artis), several poetry and prose books. Besides her scientific work published in international scientific journals (over 100 articles), three university books ("Critical Literacy", "Educational Leadership", "Educational Leadership Trainings") she writes poetry, prose and literary critics. She has published one prose book: "Coffee, Tea and the Red Sky" (2019), co-authored one poetry book for children and authored 9 poetry books: "Word about the Word" (2014), "Poems for the Margins" (2015), "Black Dot" (2017), Footprints" (2017), "Three" (2019), "House of Contrasts" (2019), "Electronic Blood" (2019), "Math Poetry" (2020) and "Walking on an Aerial Line" (2021). Her book "Electronic Blood" is translated into Arabic language by Raed Anis Al-Jishi and published by Rashawen publishing house in United Arab Emirates in 2021.

She has won special mention at the Nosside World Poetry Prize (UNESCO, 2011), the award for the best unpublished poem at the Macedonia Writers' Association Festival (2018), "Krste Chachanski" prize for prose (2019), National "Karamanov" Poetry Prize for poetry 2019, Macedonian Literary Avant-garde (2020), "Abduvali Qutbiddin" (third, 2020, Uzbekistan), Premio Mondiale "Tulliola- Renato Filippelli" in Italy (2021), International Award of Excellence "City of Galateo-Antonio De Ferraris" (Italy, Rome, 2021), and the most important national award for poetry "Aco Shopov" (by Macedonian Writers' Association in 2021 for the book "Math Poetry").

Her poetry was published in a number of anthologies, literary magazines and journals both at home and abroad, and her works are translated into more than 38 languages: English, Serbian, Slovenian, Croatian, Bosnian, Bulgarian, Albanian, Romanian, Polish, Chinese, Arabic, Turkish, Vietnamese, Uzbek, Bengali, German, Italian, French, Dutch, Spanish, German, Portuguese, Sicilian, Greek, Hindi, Japanese, Farsi, Icelandic, Russian, Filipino, Hebrew, Tamil, Bangla, Irish, Armenian, Indonesian, Malay, Catalan. She has translated many literary works from English, Serbian and Bulgarian language into Macedonian and vice versa.

Table of Contents

www.ingramcontent.com/pod-product-compliance
Lightning Source LLC
Chambersburg PA
CBHW022201160726
48282CB00024B/279
9788182537798